I0152028

Twenty-Three

— OVERCOMING UNCERTAINTY —

THROUGH GOD'S PRICELESS PROMISES

Jud Flint

Twenty-Three; Overcoming Uncertainty Through God's Priceless Promises
Copyright © 2023 by Jud Flint

Published by Clay Bridges Press in Houston, TX
www.ClayBridgesPress.com

All rights reserved. No part of this publication may be reproduced, stored in a retrieval system, or transmitted in any form by any means, electronic, mechanical, photocopy, recording, or otherwise, without the prior permission of the publisher, except as provided for by USA copyright law.

Scripture quotations marked (NIV) are taken from the Holy Bible, New International Version®, NIV®. Copyright © 1973, 1978, 1984, 2011 by Biblica, Inc.™ Used by permission of Zondervan. All rights reserved worldwide. www.zondervan.com The "NIV" and "New International Version" are trademarks registered in the United States Patent and Trademark Office by Biblica, Inc.™

Scripture quotations marked (NKJV) are taken from the New King James Version®. Copyright © 1982 by Thomas Nelson. Used by permission. All rights reserved.

Scripture quotations marked (NASB) are taken from the (NASB®) New American Standard Bible®, Copyright © 1960, 1971, 1977, 1995, 2020 by The Lockman Foundation. Used by permission. All rights reserved. www.lockman.org

Scripture quotations marked (NLT) are taken from the Holy Bible, New Living Translation, copyright © 1996, 2004, 2015 by Tyndale House Foundation. Used by permission of Tyndale House Publishers, Carol Stream, Illinois 60188. All rights reserved.

Scripture quotations marked (AMP) are taken from the Amplified Bible. Copyright © 1954, 1958, 1962, 1964, 1965, 1987 by The Lockman Foundation, La Habra, CA. All rights reserved. Used by Permission.

ISBN: 978-1-68488-064-5
eISBN: 978-1-68488-065-2

Special Sales: Most Clay Bridges titles are available in special quantity discounts. Custom imprinting or excerpting can also be done to fit special needs. Contact Clay Bridges at Info@ ClayBridgesPress.com

"Jud Flint has written an excellent work on the 23rd Psalm that opens the background to the writer and the writer's subject: The Great Shepherd. He unpacks these six powerful verses to reveal the relationship between the sheep and their loving, providing, and protecting Shepherd.

He reveals how the Good Shepherd walks with you from the valley to the victory. Every chapter is teeming with wisdom nuggets to encourage and empower you to rise from the valley and shadows and walk with the Shepherd as He leads you through the green pastures and still waters into the banquet hall and seats you at the victor's table. You will thoroughly enjoy this book."

—DR. KEN DRAUGHON, SUPERINTENDENT,
Alabama Ministry Network of the AG

"Have you ever felt overwhelmed, beaten down, or ready to quit? Hold on and read *Twenty Three*. In these pages, Jud Flint teaches you to gain the strength to continue on even if you feel you are walking through the very shadow of death yourself. *Twenty Three* is just what you need to gain the courage to finish strong."

—GREG MELVIN, LEAD PASTOR,
Safe Harbor Outreach Center, Prattville, AL

"Jud Flint, in his book *Twenty-Three*, portrays a vivid picture of one of the most loved Psalms. As you read this book you will discover that Psalms 23 is a spiritual lullaby that your Good Shepherd sings over you during every season of your life. Saturated with Scripture, truth, and revelation, Brother Flint gives clear and deep understanding into Psalms 23. You will be intrigued, instructed, and encouraged as you read this powerful book. I have such respect for Jud Flint and highly recommend this book as an excellent guide to actually applying Psalms 23 to your walk with our Precious Lord, Jesus Christ."

—REVEREND LANE SIMMONS, SENIOR PASTOR,
First Assembly of God, Greenville, AL

"As a pastor, I was moved with Jud's insight on the 23rd Psalm. It is a passionate read that personally engaged me with a deepening quest to find every golden nugget that the psalm provides for each of us, providing specific steps for honor, security, provision, happiness, and enlightenment. I consider it to be a wealth of informative insight to create a solid foundation for living our best lives today in this unstable world. It was a true joy that kept my spirit seeking more and more, page after page . . . a great gift to us all."

—LEON HALL, SENIOR PASTOR,
Faith Walk Ministries, Luverne, AL

"Rev. Jud Flint and his wife Becky had a personal journey with Psalm 23. The promises of God stood strong in their lives and remain strong. What was learned from that journey is made available for you to experience. What begins as speaking of Who our Shepherd is ends with speaking to our Shepherd. He is your personal Shepherd. Though read and quoted hundreds of times, it is like reading it for the first time with the idea, "Now I understand." This battle song of Psalm 23 will propel you into victory."

—VIRGINIA CORNETT, D.TH., ACADEMIC DEAN,
Christian Life School of Theology Global

To my girls . . .

my wife, Becky

my daughter, Hannah

To my Becca: Without you, I would have never come to love this passage of scripture that is the focus of this book. Your love for God and His Word has touched me immensely. You have blessed my life beyond the words I could put on this page. I can never thank God enough for you. Besides my salvation, the best decision of my life has been marrying you. I thank God for bringing us together. You are loving, compassionate, courageous, and kind. Thank you for "doing life" with me and also serving as my chief cheerleader, consultant, and even editor of this book. I love you—East to West.

To my daughter, Hannah: You amaze me and make me proud every . . . single . . . day. You are wise beyond your years, and your love of Jesus makes my heart happy. You are going to be a world-changer. Your heavenly Father is going to take you places that will shake hell and make heaven celebrate. Thank you for the honor of being your earthly dad. I love you, not because of what you do, what you know, or what you are going to accomplish but because of who you are. And who you are is pretty remarkable.

Contents

Introduction

It was Friday, December 25, 2009. Christmas Day had arrived. What was supposed to be a day of family, joy, and celebration was not going well. My precious wife, Becky, was having some issues that were puzzling both of us. We were in the third year of my pastoring a wonderful small church in a community that we lived in and loved. She had been in a flurry of activity that week, including taking one of our church members for an outpatient surgical procedure. However, while she was driving and then caring for the church member, she began to experience dizziness out of the blue which made it difficult for her to drive and walk. She called me, we prayed together, and she pressed on.

Becky got home that night and got some rest, but the problem didn't go away. She bravely pushed through the week—after all, it was just a few days before Christmas. Our daughter was two years old at that time. She was filled with wonder, vitality, and excitement for Santa, so we kept praying and pushing through.

Christmas Day came, and that morning Becky's symptoms got worse. Her eyesight became a bit blurry. I was concerned. She wanted to keep pushing through the morning and didn't want the focus to be on her. She wanted to focus on our daughter and the other family members we would soon be around. She wanted to get through the day and then go to a doctor.

Once we got through the early morning gift exchange at our home, we traveled a short distance to my brother and sister-in-law's house across town where all our families would join together for more celebration, food, and gift exchanges. Becky did what she had been doing all week; she persevered until her sister noticed her balance issues. Becky's eyesight became worse, and her eyes began pointing in different directions. It was then that we began getting very concerned that this issue might be serious. In the early afternoon, my wife's mother took over the care of our daughter, and Becky and I went to the emergency room in our local town. After Becky went through a few hours of tests, blood work, and a CT scan, the doctor told us they had found some abnormalities in her brain and that she needed to be transferred to a larger hospital an hour away. Since she was stable, the doctor said I could take her there without going by ambulance if we went right away. So late that Christmas afternoon, we headed in our van to Montgomery, Alabama, to another hospital where my dear wife had more tests. It was a surreal day filled with much emotion and uncertainty.

Remember, I was a pastor. My dad was a pastor. I grew up around ministry, and my faith was deep and secure. We knew the hope we had in Christ. I am not one to get shaken very easily, but in the following days, as the tests continued and the looks on the doctors' faces got more serious, I have to confess that fear began rising in my heart. It is one thing for something to be going on with me. It was quite another for something serious to be attacking the treasure God had blessed me with and designed for me to do life and ministry with. I can't begin to describe my love for her. It is deep. So I found myself trying to hold it together and be strong for both of us.

As I was trying to comfort Becky—my Becca—that week, I noticed that she continued to pray a certain scripture, Psalm 23, over and over. She endured MRI testing and whispered that scripture to the Lord in prayer. She went through a spinal tap procedure and whispered that scripture again. Complications arose from the spinal tap procedure. Her pain level skyrocketed. I felt helpless but kept crying out to God and loving on Becca. We prayed together, and she kept reciting and confessing the 23rd Psalm. It gave her comfort. It provided her solace. It helped keep her centered on her Savior and reminded her that the Great Shepherd was her shepherd, too. And it reminded me of that, too. I was supposed to be comforting her, but her whisper of that prayer—that confession of God's Word—comforted me.

That long week resulted in the doctors finding numerous active lesions on my wife's brain and a resulting diagnosis of multiple sclerosis, or MS. It was a difficult week. We were then faced with all kinds of decisions to make in the days ahead to treat her condition. We shed a lot of tears. And we did what we had always done since the day we were married—we kept holding on to each other while reaching out to our Lord for direction, healing, and wisdom. That confession of scripture in prayer that Becky whispered continually reminded us to do that.

As a pastor and longtime Christian, I knew the 23rd Psalm. I had heard sermons that referenced various parts of those six simple verses. I had heard it used in funerals many times. I had often referenced that scripture in my sermons as well. But honestly, I had never thought deeply about the words in that psalm. It was a scripture I knew but not a scripture that had become part of me. That began to change.

Fast forward a decade of life and ministry to 2019. I was praying and reading the Word of God one week, and the Holy Spirit deeply impressed on me to go back to that psalm. The Holy Spirit reminded me how it had sustained us 10 years before. I was convicted that there was more to this passage of scripture that I needed to understand. So I read it again . . . and again . . . and again. Each time, my heart burned with more intensity. I began studying it and meditating on it while asking the God of the Word to open up this scripture to me. I wanted to understand truly why it had carried us through all those years ago. I wanted to comprehend why I had never been able to pass by this passage without it unusually captivating my heart. I wanted God to unpack this psalm in my mind and brand it irrevocably on my heart and soul. That journey resulted in this book.

My life has been forever changed by swimming in the precious pool of the six verses of this powerful prose penned by the heart of a shepherd under the inspiration of the God he wrote about. He had the understanding and revelation that I desperately longed for. Thus began a journey—a journey I am all the better for taking. It is a journey that has given me sustaining joy amid deep sorrow. These promises of God have provided me with strength when I felt weak. I have been given perspective when I couldn't really see what would be around the next corner. These promises have fueled my faith and life even during great loss.

I didn't know that also in 2019 when God took me on this journey of discovery into this scripture passage, my personal mentor and the man who led me to faith in Christ—my dad—would take his journey to heaven that summer. I didn't know, but God knew. The Good Shepherd knew what I needed. Since that time, my family has walked through many valleys and shadows. We have seen God do mighty things, as well as share in the loss of those we held so dear. And yet through every shadow and valley, we found ourselves not getting weaker. We didn't lose our footing, and we certainly didn't lose our faith or our way. Rather we found strength, help, guidance, and hope in the arms and promises of the Great Shepherd found in the six verses of Psalm 23 that we will soon unpack and explore together.

Friends, I have found valuable promises from the God of the universe on this road. They have comforted me, sustained me, and propelled me forward in hope through some very dark days in my life and in the life of my family. I deeply love this passage of scripture. It is powerful.

I want you to love and feel its power as I do. Today I understand why my Becca kept whispering these words. I know why it mattered. I know why it helped. And I want you to know, too. I know your time is important. I am honored that you took some of that precious time to pick up this book. I won't waste your time, I promise you.

Let's start our journey through a passage of scripture that many think they know but, like me, need to go on a deeper expedition into its profound meaning.

Let's take this journey together.

I believe it will be well worth your time.

Chapter One

A Life Song Written by a Shepherd Who Became King

The Lord is my shepherd;
I shall not want.
He makes me to lie down in green pastures;
He leads me beside the still waters.
He restores my soul;
He leads me in the paths of righteousness
For His name's sake.

Yea, though I walk through the valley of the shadow of death,
I will fear no evil;
For You are *with me;*
Your rod and Your staff, they comfort me.

You prepare a table before me in the presence of my enemies;
You anoint my head with oil;
My cup runs over.
Surely goodness and mercy shall follow me
All the days of my life;
And I will dwell in the house of the Lord
Forever.

—PS. 23:1–6

This is a very powerful scripture indeed. Besides John 3:16, this passage of scripture is likely the most well-known and oft-quoted in the entire Bible. The great 19th-century prince of preachers Charles Spurgeon called it "the pearl of psalms."[1] It has been referenced and called upon many times on many occasions, especially in times of trouble when life gets difficult and the bends of life become sharp and hard to navigate. This potent psalm provides comfort, peace, and hope to those who soak in the pool of its life-giving words.

It is a psalm—a song—attributed to the shepherd boy who would become king. His name was David. In fact, his kingship would become the high watermark of every man to sit on the throne of Israel, even using his name to point to a King from heaven Who would proceed from his line and take the reign that David started into eternal perpetuity. Yes, the Son of God would also be known as the Son of David.

We do not know the occasion for which David wrote this psalm or the time of his life when he penned the words on parchment, but many have their opinions. Some scholars and Bible commentators think it was written while he was young—as a shepherd boy in the fields forging a deep and what would become lasting personal and passionate relationship with the God of the universe. But a great many scholars—and I throw my meager hat in with theirs—believe these words were written by David in the sunset years of his life. It seems to be written from a long, reflective look back rather than a prospective look forward. To me, this notion seems to fit the best.

Professor and author Haddon Robinson wrote:

> David was a mature man, filled with his share of the conflicting passions and confusing problems that confront any human being. Not only was he the heroic slayer of Goliath, the devoted friend of Jonathan, lover of music, and an able king, but he was also a haggard fugitive, an adulterer and a murderer. . . . As a father he had watched his baby die, and had wept when his ungrateful son Absalom was slain as he led an armed rebellion

---

1. Charles H. Spurgeon, *The Treasury of David*, The Spurgeon Archive, accessed October 21, 2022, https://archive.spurgeon.org/treasury/ps023.php#:~:text=This%20is%20the%20pearl%20 of,and%20its%20spirituality%20are%20unsurpassed.

against his father. David has not left us with only beautiful thoughts, but with an honest testimony about God learned while living life to the hilt.[2]

I see this psalm as a deep and powerful ballad of a man who had deeply drunk the dregs of life and tasted and seen extensively.

As a man who had been young but now was old, it was written as a reflection of his storied life. From the frolicking days of early childhood to the days in the fields as a young shepherd, to the days of serving faithfully under Saul, to facing Goliath, to running for his life from a jealous king and hiding in caves, to the days of his kingship and all the days thereafter with Bathsheba, Uriah, Amnon, and Absalom—all the days of victory and even the agony of seasons of defeat—he is reflecting on his life and now understands "something of the depth of the Lord's care."[3]

David was a man who had truly seen it all. He faced an empty belly and a full stomach. He learned to navigate through ravenous days of famine and had to find a way to keep his eyes on God through pervading pestilent disease. David lived through more things than 10 Louis L'Amour novels. He enjoyed the warmth of the fullness of love and faced the coldness of being stabbed deeply by the knife of betrayal. He watched those he loved die and faced the hardened glare of the shadow of death on more than one occasion.

Yet through it all, one thing remained constant—this deep relationship with his God that he had forged on the back side of a pasture while herding sheep. He even forged his own instruments and made it his life's habit to worship this God he came to know. It would prove to be the deepest and most abiding passion of his life. The love song of his life was not his women. It wasn't his children, it wasn't the things he amassed, and it wasn't the kingly power he grasped in his well-calloused

---

2. Haddon W. Robinson, *The Good Shepherd* (Chicago: Moody Press, 1968), 11–12.

3. *The Preacher's Outline & Sermon Bible (POSB)* (Chattanooga: Leadership Ministries Worldwide), Copyright 1991, 1996, 2004 by Alpha-Omega Ministries, Inc., WORDsearch Bible Library Electronic Database, accessed December 15, 2022, (Psalm 23 Commentary).

hands. The deepest chord of the melody of his life song was found in the love of a relationship he had come to know with his God . . . a personal God . . . his God. And now as the sun was setting on his life, this man who became king was penning what may very well be the grandest opus of his life. It is what we have come to know as the 23rd Psalm.

This psalm has come to mean a great deal to me. It penetrates the very depths of my soul. I have come to treasure every word since it speaks volumes about my journey in life. I want to take some time and ponder this powerful song with you.

Let's not rush. Let's take our time and breathe it in, verse by precious verse. Let's reflect on and deeply drink from the reservoir of six verses that can change our lives if we dare to pause and allow them to become rooted and planted deep within our souls.

Come along on this journey with me. Together let's go deeper as we ponder the power of the priceless promises proclaimed in the 23rd Psalm.

Notes

Chapter Two

A Personal Shepherd for a Personal Journey

Let's start our journey by examining every word, beginning with the first verse.

> *The Lord is my shepherd; I shall not want.*
>
> —PS. 23:1

> *The Lord is my Shepherd [to feed, guide, and shield me], I shall not lack.*
>
> —PS. 23:1 (AMPC)

The Lord Is My Shepherd
In the first verse of Psalm 23, notice the first two words—"The Lord." You might see the word *Lord* fully capitalized if you have a King James Version (KJV) or New King James Version (NKJV) of the Bible. Thus, the word Lord means Yahweh.

David then is not referring to a god but to *the* GOD. He is referring to the God of the universe and of Israel. He is referring to Yahweh—the I AM, the self-existent, eternal One. He is the One who always was, always is, and always will be. He formed the world out of the expanse of the greatness of His mind's eye.

This world that we live in, this grand scenery that we take in with our senses, is all God's invention—His creation. He called the seas into existence. This firmament we call land and build empires upon, the

I AM called it into existence. Every tree, every flower, every animal, every mountain peak above, and every valley below, Yahweh called it forth with His life-giving breath. He is the God to who all things answer for He is the Creator of all things. He . . . is . . . God.

When David wrote "the Lord," he was writing the name the Jews thought was too holy even to say. He is God; He is the Lord; He is Yahweh. He was; He is, and He always will be.

Then David Says "My Shepherd"

If you have a KJV OR NKJV Bible, you will see that the word *is*, is italicized. That means the word was added to try to provide a continuous phrase, but it is not in the original Hebrew manuscript. Thus, the phrase David actually wrote was "Yahweh—my shepherd.

The word *shepherd* in Hebrew is *Roh'i* (or *Ra'a*). It is one of the names of God in the Old Testament. Yahweh Roh'i, the Lord, my Shepherd.

David is picking up a theme that many before him had noted—that God was a shepherd to His people. However, for David, this name was a concept that he understood very well. His first vocation was as a shepherd. He knew what a shepherd was and what a shepherd did. After all, that is where he really began to seek God out, and then it became the place where God picked him out. He was hand-picked by God through an old seer prophet named Samuel. David was called out of a sheepfold on the back side of a wilderness to answer the call of God on his life. Friends, David knew this word *shepherd*.

Let's now understand it better together (like David did).

Shepherd (Hebrew: *Roh'i*):

This Shepherd guides me; this Shepherd protects me. The Shepherd is always there (*Jehovah Shammah*). He is *always* there. Never *ever* will He leave me.

I am reminded of the Word of God in Deuteronomy.

> *Be strong and of good courage, do not fear nor be afraid of them; for the Lord your God, He is the One who goes with you. He will not leave you nor forsake you.*
>
>   —DEUT. 31:6

> *The eternal God is your refuge,*
> *And underneath are the everlasting arms;*
> *He will thrust out the enemy from before you,*
> *And will say, "Destroy!"*
>
>   —DEUT. 33:27

Yes! He is the Shepherd who . . .

- ✓ Feeds me
- ✓ Guides me
- ✓ Protects me
- ✓ Shields me
- ✓ Loves and cares for me

He is the Shepherd who is . . .

- ✓ My supplier
- ✓ My protector
- ✓ My direction—my way
- ✓ Everything to me

He is *the* Shepherd.

And I . . . I am a sheep.

I must humble myself before the Shepherd and feel my need. I can't do this thing called life on my own. Why?

Because as a sheep . . .

- I am prone to do foolish things
- I can be stubborn
- I can find myself defenseless
- I am prone to wander
- I am slow to recognize danger
- I can easily deceive myself
- I can be nervous and uneasy
- I am easily excitable and frightened at times[4]

So in this first verse, we see God named. We see Him called the Shepherd. And further, we see a possessive note. Jehovah Roh'i is *my* Shepherd. I see now that this is a personal thing. He is not just *the* Shepherd. He certainly is the Shepherd, but this life is personal. For this to work in my life, He has to be, He has to become *my* Shepherd.

Jesus died and rose again for me. He is *my* Shepherd. This is a deeply personal journey, and that's okay. It should be that way for He is a deeply personal God.

Further, He is a detailed God. After all, He made dandelions and sunflowers. He painted the tulip and the rose. He cascades the mountaintops with pristine snow. He made the lion and the lamb. He made every snowflake with a little different twist. He painted this world with color and majestic beauty. He is a detailed God who knows every detail of this creation He has made.

He also made you and me with great detail. He called us a masterpiece.

> *For we are God's masterpiece. He has created us anew in Christ Jesus, so we can do the good things he planned for us long ago.*
>
> —EPH. 2:10 (NLT)

---

4. Paraphrased from *The Preacher's Outline & Sermon Bible (POSB)* (Chattanooga: Leadership Ministries Worldwide), Copyright 1991, 1996, 2004 by Alpha-Omega Ministries, Inc., WORDsearch Bible Library Electronic Database, accessed December 15, 2022, (Psalm 23 Commentary).

You and I were designed by a Master Designer with a master plan in mind by the God who calls forth and declares the end from the beginning and from ancient times, things that are not yet done (Isa. 46:10). He is a detailed God who is concerned with my details. After all, that is why God became flesh and became the God who would live among us.

> *And the Word became flesh and dwelt among us, and we beheld His glory, the glory as of the only begotten of the Father, full of grace and truth.*
> —JOHN 1:14

God is detailed, and He is personal. He is not elusive. And He is surely not feckless. Nor is He absent in mind or in presence. His strength is without limit, and His knowledge is without bounds. He has no weakness, and there is no mark He cannot hit. The only two things He cannot do is lie or fail. Everything else is within His grasp and power.

Mankind cannot outthink Him; the devil could not defeat Him; death could not hold Him; and the grave couldn't keep Him. And surely that grave did its best to keep Him down. It was to be the one finality of life—the great equalizer of all people. Yet when it was time, the One who laid His life down took it back up again. And because of His resurrection, He is without a loss and is now the grand champion of all eternity.

He thus cannot be outmatched, outdone, or overdone, and no one can undo what He has done. His presence is always available, and His love cannot be extinguished. That is not to say that mankind hasn't tried. Yet in doing so, he has only found that God's mercy is new as the dew every morning and His love like a bubbling spring that comes from a reservoir that has no end. And this God—this Savior—He is *my* Shepherd. That is who He is. I am His, and He is mine, and His banner over me is love (Song of Sol. 2:4).

That covers the first phrase of the first verse—"The Lord *is* my shepherd." Oh, what a powerful phrase that is! Now let's look at the next part of that first verse.

I shall not want.

We must understand that David is not saying he didn't have needs. That is not what this phrase means. It doesn't mean that you and I don't have needs. We surely do. Every day a new need pops up. It also doesn't mean we don't have problems. We have those too. And sometimes, on some days, it seems like problems surround us and try to take the very breath from our lungs.

This, then, is not some pat phrase or breezy declaration without thought or depth. It is much grander and goes much deeper.

Because the Lord is my Shepherd, He is with me. And further, He is not a hireling shepherd. Jesus made the distinction.

> *I am the good shepherd. The good shepherd gives His life for the sheep. But a hireling, he who is not the shepherd, one who does not own the sheep, sees the wolf coming and leaves the sheep and flees; and the wolf catches the sheep and scatters them. The hireling flees because he is a hireling and does not care about the sheep. I am the good shepherd; and I know My sheep, and am known by My own. As the Father knows Me, even so I know the Father; and I lay down My life for the sheep.*
> —JOHN 10:11–15

A hireling shepherd is just in it for the paycheck. And when the going gets tough, the hireling gets going. A hireling will flee and let the sheep scatter. He will abandon the sheep if it means his own skin getting in a bind.

But the Good Shepherd is no hireling. He is the Shepherd who owns the sheep. He paid the ultimate price for the sheep. His price was bathed in His perfect and precious blood. He gave His life for the sheep. He knows His sheep and is known by them. He is like the shepherds of old who care for their sheep's every need. He is the shepherd who helps his sheep give birth, feeds them, protects them, guides them, rescues them, and disciplines them when they stray—knowing that their hope of life grows very dim indeed without them by His powerful side. He is the Shepherd who lives among His sheep. He is Jesus, Emmanuel—the God who is *with* us!

Thus this Shepherd is there. He never goes off duty. His presence is with the sheep.

Because His presence is there, all that He is and all that He has is *with* Him.

Again, this is a personal thing. My Shepherd knows me. He knows what I have and what I don't have. He knows my fears, my weaknesses, my strengths, my failures, and my pros and cons. He knows it all, and yet He still wants to hang out with me. He knows it all, and He still loves me, calling me by name.

> But now, thus says the Lord, who created you, O Jacob, And He who formed you, O Israel: "Fear not, for I have redeemed you; I have called you by your name; You are Mine."
>
> —ISA. 43:1

Because He is there, I do not lack. That is how the word *want* is translated. It is from the Hebrew word *haser* (pronounced khaw-sare') and can mean lack, want, fail, decrease, abate, bereave, need, make lower.[5]

In this context, the words mean because, and as long as the Lord is my Shepherd—I shall not want, lack, fail, or have need. He will feed me. He will guide me. He will shield me. He will protect me. This Great and Good Shepherd will provide what I need.

> Therefore I say to you, do not worry about your life, what you will eat or what you will drink; nor about your body, what you will put on. Is not life more than food and the body more than clothing? Look at the birds of the

5. James Strong, *Strong's Talking Greek and Hebrew Dictionary* (WORDsearch, 2020) (Strong's 2637), WORDsearch Bible Library Electronic Database, accessed December 15, 2022.

air, for they neither sow nor reap nor gather into barns; yet your heavenly Father feeds them. Are you not of more value than they? Which of you by worrying can add one cubit to his stature? So why do you worry about clothing? Consider the lilies of the field, how they grow: they neither toil nor spin; and yet I say to you that even Solomon in all his glory was not arrayed like one of these. Now if God so clothes the grass of the field, which today is, and tomorrow is thrown into the oven, will He not much more clothe you, O you of little faith? Therefore do not worry, saying, "What shall we eat?" or "What shall we drink?" or "What shall we wear?" For after all these things the Gentiles seek. For your heavenly Father knows that you need all these things. But seek first the kingdom of God and His righteousness, and all these things shall be added to you.

—MATT. 6:25–33

I have been young, and now am old;
Yet I have not seen the righteous forsaken,
Nor his descendants begging bread.

—PS. 37:25

The Great Shepherd has promised to take care of me. He has promised to keep me from lack. That means . . .

- ✓ I won't lack bread.
- ✓ I won't lack drink.
- ✓ I won't lack any good thing.

That includes . . .

- ✓ Peace for my restlessness
- ✓ Strength for my weakness
- ✓ Light for my darkness
- ✓ Vision to rightly navigate the road before me

I shall not want. I will have what I need. Why? Because He is here with me. And when He is here, all of heaven's resources come with the King of Heaven. When I realize that, I realize that His presence is truly heaven. And when I have Him, I realize I have it all. And because He is with me, because He is near, because He is present, I don't need a thing. If I have Him—then I have everything I need.

He is my portion. He is my joy. He is. And He is mine.

This first verse, then, is a confession.

- It is a confession that the Lord is *my* Shepherd (this is personal).
- It is a confession of who He is and my personal, humble awareness and confession of my need.

It is then a confession that He is the Shepherd, He is *my* Shepherd, and I am a sheep that needs Him. And because I am aware of that need and reach out to Him by faith, this Great and Good Shepherd will come to me and be mine.

He is with me. And because of His very near and precious presence that is with and in me, I am not just okay—I am good. When I am with Him, He rubs off on me. His goodness gets in me. I am good because He is good. He's even better than I thought.

The Lord is *my Shepherd; I shall not want.*

There is much in that first verse.

The only question now as we conclude this chapter is simply this. Have you made the Great and Good Shepherd *your* Shepherd?

His promises only stand for those who are His—those who have entered the door of His sheepfold. And Jesus is that door.

> *Then Jesus said to them again, "Most assuredly, I say to you, I am the door of the sheep."*
>
> —JOHN 10:7

I am the door. If anyone enters by Me, he will be saved, and will go in and out and find pasture.

—JOHN 10:9

The precious and permanent promises found in this 23rd Psalm are found by the sheep who enter through Jesus.

Might I have permission to get a little personal with you? Would you take a minute and look into the depths of your soul and ask yourself the following questions?

This Great and Good Shepherd—Jesus Christ—have you made Him your Shepherd? Have you asked Him into your heart and life and asked Him to shepherd your life?

If you have not, might I lead you in a prayer to do that very thing right now?

Dear Heavenly Father,
My life needs a Shepherd. I have tried to lead and control my own life, and it really hasn't worked out so well. I need help. I need You! I have made many mistakes. I have failed many times. I acknowledge these mistakes and failures as sins. I need forgiveness. I am in desperate need of the grace You offer through Your Son, Jesus. So right now, I confess every failure and sin of my life, and I admit that my best will never be good enough. I repent of my sins and humbly ask for Your forgiveness and grace to save me. Forgive me, Lord. Save me right now in this very moment. I place my life in Your hands and ask for the Great and Good Shepherd—Jesus—to become my Shepherd. Thank you, Father. By faith, I receive this salvation. Amen.

Let us enter in and taste every good thing the Great and Good Shepherd offers. You just started on that journey. It is a journey of salvation that includes forgiveness for your past, a purpose for your present, and promises you can stand upon for your future. The Great and Good Shepherd is *your* shepherd now! Hallelujah! That is exciting!

Notes

Chapter Three

The Shepherd Who Leads, Restores, and Provides

We are on a marvelous journey. We are unpacking the 23rd Psalm verse by verse to discover why it is so poignant, precious, and powerful. Let's take a moment and read this entire psalm again together.

The Lord is my shepherd;
I shall not want.
He makes me to lie down in green pastures;
He leads me beside the still waters.
He restores my soul;
He leads me in the paths of righteousness
For His name's sake.

Yea, though I walk through the valley of the shadow of death,
I will fear no evil;
For You are with me;
Your rod and Your staff, they comfort me.

You prepare a table before me in the presence of my enemies;
You anoint my head with oil;
My cup runs over.
Surely goodness and mercy shall follow me
All the days of my life;
And I will dwell in the house of the Lord
Forever.

—PS. 23:1–6

Remember that we started looking at this psalm by examining its writer, David. These are the writings and reflections of a man who had faced the steely eyes of lions and bears and defeated them in the wilderness. He had no cell phone to call for help or a high-powered rifle to put them down. He had only the tools of the shepherd—the rod and the staff, the club and the crook—and he used them well. This young shepherd forged a deep and lasting relationship with a powerful God on the backside of a wilderness while tending sheep. And as he progressed through the twists and turns of life, even being exalted to the highest place a man could attain—the royal place of a king—David's heartstring was always attached to the God who called him by name so many years ago.

David had tasted the best and choicest morsels this world had to offer. He had the best and most sought-after wines. He also experienced deep hunger because he had nothing to eat. His stomach had known hunger. He had lived like a vagabond, being forced to hide and scrounge around in caves. He is an old man now, and he had walked the hallowed and highest halls that were considered the pinnacles of success. He had also been dragged through the lowest and most barren valleys. His one constant companion through it all proved to be his God. The deepest chord of the melody of his life was not his wives, it wasn't his children, nor was it the kingdom that was built around him. The deepest chord of the melody of his life was found in the love of a relationship he had come to know with his God. And this God had carried him through every twist and turn he had faced.

This psalm we are looking at was penned by someone who knew something of what he was talking about.

In the previous chapter of this book, we looked at the key that opens the lock to the entire six verses. It is the first verse—a declaration and confession. It is David's declaration that the Lord, Jehovah, is his Shepherd. He is the God of the universe and knows His sheep by name. David was alluding to the vast expanse of the God who knew him and the God he had spent a lifetime coming to know. And it was a confession—a confession that if God is the great, good, and, yes, chief Shepherd, then he is a sheep in need of the Shepherd's presence, guidance, care, and protection. The first verse, then, was a declaration of who God is and David's personal, humble awareness and confession of his need. And because of that declaration and confession, David declared that he would not want or lack.

With this in mind, let's look now at the next two verses and see how they are tied to the first. Let's read them again.

> The Lord is *my shepherd;*
> *I shall not want.*
> *He makes me to lie down in green pastures;*
> *He leads me beside the still waters.*
> *He restores my soul;*
> *He leads me in the paths of righteousness*
> *For His name's sake.*
>
> —PS. 23:1–2

Green pastures and still waters . . . I love the imagery here. It is a serene picture of provision and peace.

Because the Lord is my Shepherd, He will make me lie down in green pastures.

Why does He have to make me lie down? *Because I might not do it on my own.*

When life is screaming in my ears and I can't hear . . . when I am disoriented in vision and my ears are ringing to the point I can't hear clearly . . . when the pressure of what I am going through is too much for me . . . I have a tendency to scuttle around in activity that matches my unrest and uncertainty. You can move around and kick up a bunch of dust and not accomplish a thing. That is what we tend to do when life is pressing in from all sides. We actually resemble the story of Chicken Little who could not stop crying out that the sky is falling.

It is hard *not* to see the problems that lurk all around us. Yet because the Lord is my Shepherd, He grabs me by the hand and makes me lie down. He stops me in my tracks and provides a place for me in His presence to lie down. It is only here in this place that I will find rest.

Where does He make me lie down? In green pastures. This is a place of provision.

The first thought here is that God will lead me to a place of provision for my needs—my physical needs.

A good shepherd is constantly looking for the right place for his sheep. It is a place where the grass is lush and green and where they can graze. He makes sure their temporal needs are taken care of.

A good shepherd will not only find a good place for the sheep to graze, but he will make sure the streams they drink from are not too rough. I found some information in my reading that a good shepherd would even take some rocks and dam off part of a brook so the water would become still and more peaceful and the sheep would be less likely to be disturbed and spooked. Why is that important?

Sheep by nature are jittery and easily excitable. They don't rest easily but rather cut and run at any sign of trouble. The problem is that when they do, they don't usually make good decisions. They run first and think second. This is not a good combination. It usually leads to more problems.

I can relate. I bet you can, too.

The Good Shepherd doesn't drive the sheep. Rather He leads the sheep and takes them to a place where they are provided for.

This is the place the Good Shepherd will take us, too, if we let Him.

David is saying that he found God to be the Good Shepherd who provides for His sheep's physical needs. God tells us the same thing. Look with me at some of these promises.

For your Father knows the things you have need of before you ask Him.
—MATT. 6:8

Therefore I say to you, do not worry about your life, what you will eat or what you will drink; nor about your body, what you will put on. Is not life more than food and the body more than clothing? Look at the birds of the air, for they neither sow nor reap nor gather into barns; yet your heavenly Father feeds them. Are you not of more value than they? Which of you by worrying can add one cubit to his stature? So why do you worry about clothing? Consider the lilies of the field, how they grow: they neither toil nor spin; and yet I say to you that even Solomon in all his glory was not arrayed like one of these. Now if God so clothes the grass of the field, which today is, and tomorrow is thrown into the oven, will He not much more clothe you, O you of little faith? Therefore do not worry saying, "What shall we eat?" or "What shall we drink?" or "What shall we wear?" For after all these things the Gentiles seek. For your heavenly Father knows that you need all these things. But seek first the kingdom of God and His righteousness, and all these things shall be added to you.
—MATT. 6:25–33

And my God shall supply all your need according to His riches in glory by Christ Jesus.
—PHIL. 4:19

Oh, fear the Lord, you His saints! There is no want to those who fear Him. The young lions lack and suffer hunger; But those who seek the Lord shall not lack any good thing.
—PS. 34:9–10

I have been young, and now am old; Yet I have not seen the righteous forsaken, Nor his descendants begging bread.
—PS. 37:25

These are promises we can and must stand on. Might I even encourage you to confess them over your life?

The Lord, your Shepherd, will lead you and grab you and *cause* you (if need be) to lie down in green pastures. This is first a place of provision.

It is also a ***place of rest.***

This place is not only a place where I can eat and be satisfied, but it is also a place where I feel safe enough to rest. Here He provides a place of rest and peace.

> *He makes me lie down in [fresh, tender] green pastures; He leads me beside the still and restful waters.*
>
> —PS. 23:2 (AMPC)

This place of green pastures comes from a Hebrew word that literally means a "pleasant place."[6] The place where the Good Shepherd leads us is a place of rest, stillness, and peace—it is a habitation of peace.

> *You will keep him in perfect peace,*
> *Whose mind is stayed on You,*
> *Because he trusts in You.*
>
> —ISA. 26:3

Let me go further. This place, then, is not just talking about my physical needs. It is going much deeper and talking about what my soul needs. David makes sure we don't miss that, so he comes right out and states it in verse three.

---

6. James Strong, *Strong's Talking Greek and Hebrew Dictionary* (WORDsearch, 2020) (Strong's 4999), WORDsearch Bible Library Electronic Database, accessed December 15, 2022.

He refreshes and restores my life (my self); He leads me in the paths of right-
eousness [uprightness and right standing with Him—not for my earning
it, but] for His name's sake.

—PS. 23:3 (AMPC)

Now the second thought comes bubbling forth.

This place that the Good Shepherd will lead me is not only a place of provision for my needs.

He is leading me into a place of provision for my soul.

This place is one of restoration and refreshment. The word *restore* means not only to return or turn back but also to bring back, recover, or carry back.[7]

God is not only the God who will lead me to a place of provision of soul rest. He will bring me back and carry me if need be. He is not only the God who calls you back; He is the God who brings you back.

It is a place for your soul. This word *soul* is the Hebrew word *nephesh*, which relates to our soul life—our mind, heart, and the desires deep within. It is our inner life. It is the life of the mind and heart. This is the place that can really drive and control us if we are not careful.

This Good Shepherd is my retreat. He will bring me back to a place of restoration and refreshment. He breathes His life into me. He not only delivers me but brings me back to a place of life and vitality. This place is a place of contentment. It comes from the reassuring presence of someone strong and mighty.

Trust in the Lord forever, For in Yah, the Lord, is everlasting strength.

—ISA. 26:4

---

7. Ibid. (Strong's 7725), accessed December 15, 2022.

When I was a kid, sometimes I had nightmares. I remember a few of them very distinctly to this day. One such time was when we were living in a rural town called Ringgold, Georgia. We lived in a two-story home surrounded by 10 acres of wood. The house had three bedrooms. My brother and I shared one of them. His bed was by the window. Mine was across the room in front of the door leading out of the room. One night, the darkness in that room and the entire house seemed so thick that you could have only cut it with a very sharp knife. I don't remember a lot about the dream that caused me to become so scared, but I do remember how terrified I was when I awoke. It was real to me. I could hear my brother sleeping in the bed that was just a few feet from me, but it seemed like a vast divide that could not be spanned. I loved my older brother, and our bond has always been close. But that night, that dark terrible night when I awoke from a vision where I knew an enemy was coming after me to take me away forever, my brother's presence wasn't enough. If that enemy could take me, he could get my brother, too. I felt too weak to even cry out. My voice felt like it was gone; it seemed barely like a squeak.

I knew what I needed to do. I had to get to my father's bedroom. It was there and only there that I would find peace, safety, and rest. I also knew I had to muster the strength to run to him. And at that moment, I had to make a decision. Would I let the darkness take my breath away, paralyze me, and overcome me, or would I run to safety? I agonized over it for what seemed like hours but was probably only minutes. If I was going to make it through the night, I knew I had to try. So with the strength I had left, I made the decision to bolt out of bed and run to the one I knew was powerful enough to defeat my enemy. I ran to the presence of my father. I didn't wake him up that night. I didn't need to because when I ran into that room and saw him sleeping, my fear instantly left. I could hear Mom and Dad sleeping, and they were at complete peace and rest. I knew the enemy would not touch me as long as I stayed in the presence of my father. So I just curled up on the floor next to his bed, and there I slept in perfect peace—at least until he almost stepped on me the next morning.

Friends, I knew my father could defeat my enemy that night. And when I ran to his presence, I knew the darkness would no longer pierce my heart. You must understand that it was still just as dark around me. I didn't turn on a light. But because of his presence, the darkness ceased to be scary anymore. Because I trusted my good father, I knew I would be just fine.

This is what I think of when I read this passage.

David is not saying that the Good Shepherd takes the darkness away. He is saying that because the Lord—the good, good Father of heaven's armies—is his Shepherd, as long as he is in His presence, He will bring him into a habitation of peace and rest despite the darkness. Even though hell's armies are screaming from all sides—even though the crisis is still not over—the Good Shepherd's presence ushers in life and peace.

We are content as long as the Shepherd is near.

I am now reminded of Paul who wrote a letter when he was locked away in prison for no real crime except serving God faithfully. He penned a letter to the believers in a city called Philippi. It is now the book of Philippians in the Bible.

> *But whatever was to my profit I now consider loss for the sake of Christ. What is more, I consider everything a loss compared to the surpassing greatness of knowing Christ Jesus my Lord, for whose sake I have lost all things. I consider them rubbish, that I may gain Christ and be found in him, not having a righteousness of my own that comes from the law, but that which is through faith in Christ—the righteousness that comes from God and is by faith. I want to know Christ and the power of his resurrection and the fellowship of sharing in his sufferings, becoming like him in his death, and so, somehow, to attain to the resurrection from the dead.*
>
> —PHIL. 3:7–11 (NIV)

Here is one more excerpt from that letter.

> *I am not saying this because I am in need, for I have learned to be content whatever the circumstances. I know what it is to be in need, and I know what it is to have plenty. I have learned the secret of being content in any and every situation, whether well fed or hungry, whether living in plenty or in want. I can do everything through him who gives me strength.*
>
> —PHIL. 4:11–13 (NIV)

Do you know what Paul is saying? He is saying that he has found a relationship with God who changed everything. It changed the entire course of his life. And all he wants to do is habitually host His presence, know Him more, and serve at the breath of His command. For as long as he had God, Paul would be just fine. His place of contentment was not in the food he ate or the clothes he wore, nor was it in the position or plaudits that people could give him. He no longer cared for human appraisals or applause. He only lived for the applause of the God of heaven.

So Paul learned a secret. He lived in contentment with much or little in each and every situation that arose, whether he was well fed or hungry, whether he was living in plenty or in want. Paul knew that as long as Christ was near, He would take care of him. And even when hell had a hit order out on him, Paul could sleep the sleep of the righteous in perfect peace.

> *When you lie down, you will not be afraid; Yes, you will lie down and your sleep will be sweet.*
>
> —PROV. 3:24

Paul had found green pastures and still waters. He found restoration and refreshment for his soul in a dank prison cell because the Lord, His Shepherd, was near. And as long as he could hear His breath nearby, the darkness had no power.

I know that feeling. I first felt it as a first grader in the town of Ringgold, Georgia, in the presence of my dad. I have since felt it many times as an adult in dark situations with my Savior who sent me His Spirit to provide me whatever I needed to not just get by but to flourish. He restores my soul. He'll restore yours as well.

Let's look at the rest of verse 3.

He leads me in the paths of righteousness.

And because He is near me, because His presence is in me, around me, and even singing over me (Zeph. 3:17), I will follow His lead. He will lead me to the right paths for my life.

He will lead me in rightness in my living and in my direction.

As I walk with the One who leads me, the darkness has to bow, and His peace comes flooding into the deepest recesses of my soul. My soul sings a new song in the very presence of my enemies, and I walk the right path despite their shouts and taunts. Their best is of no avail when I trust and lean on the Lord my Shepherd. His path is right. It is a path that is in step with His nature and brings honor to His name and life.

I have learned that I will prosper as my soul prospers.

> *Beloved, I pray that you may prosper in all things and be in health, just as your soul prospers.*
> —3 JOHN 1:2

And my soul will prosper if I am living not from humans' bread but by the proceeding word of the living God, the Great Shepherd of my soul.

> *But He answered and said, "It is written, 'Man shall not live by bread alone, but by every word that proceeds from the mouth of God.'"*
> —MATT. 4:4

Thank God for the Shepherd who makes the darkness tremble and silences all fear. His name cannot be overcome. His name is life and light. His name is the name that all heaven stands at attention to and to whom every knee will bow. His name is Jesus, and He is our Shepherd.

And because He is our Shepherd, we will lie down in green pastures. We will then drink from still waters. Even when we become frantic, He will put His arms around us and set us on our feet, calm our fears, and cause us to rest in the place of His habitation. It is a place where not only our needs are met but where our souls find rest and peace. This is a great consolation in a world that provides nothing but broken promises and fleeting hope.

Our Shepherd's promises are sure, and His hope cannot be extinguished. He is! And He has me!

Let Him have you, too, beloved.

He is the Good Shepherd. He will lead you into green pastures and peaceful streams. He will bring life, vitality, restoration, and even utter contentment to your soul. He will lead you in the right paths for the honor of His wonderful name and your precious gain.

All you have to do is lean in, take Him by the hand, declare that He is your Shepherd, and dare to trust His promises. They never fail.

Let us build our lives on His promises.

> *Therefore everyone who hears these words of mine and puts them into practice is like a wise man who built his house on the rock. The rain came down, the streams rose, and the winds blew and beat against that house; yet it did not fall, because it had its foundation on the rock. But everyone who hears these words of mine and does not put them into practice is like a foolish man who built his house on sand. The rain came down, the*

streams rose, and the winds blew and beat against that house, and it fell
with a great crash.

—MATT. 7:24–27

Let us choose to build our lives on His words and His promises. David
found assurance, peace, rest, and provision in the Good Shepherd's
care. Those promises are just as valid for us.

He lets me rest in green meadows;
he leads me beside peaceful streams.
He renews my strength.
He guides me along right paths,
bringing honor to his name.

—PS. 23:2–3 (NLT)

What a Shepherd! He . . . is . . . good!

Notes

Chapter Four

The Shepherd, the Shadows, and Your Personal Valleys

Let's take a look at Psalm 23 again.

> *The Lord* is *my shepherd;*
> *I shall not want.*
> *He makes me to lie down in green pastures;*
> *He leads me beside the still waters.*
> *He restores my soul;*
> *He leads me in the paths of righteousness*
> *For His name's sake.*
>
> *Yea, though I walk through the valley of the shadow of death,*
> *I will fear no evil;*
> *For You* are *with me;*
> *Your rod and Your staff, they comfort me.*
>
> *You prepare a table before me in the presence of my enemies;*
> *You anoint my head with oil;*
> *My cup runs over.*
> *Surely goodness and mercy shall follow me*
> *All the days of my life;*
> *And I will dwell in the house of the Lord*
> *Forever.*

—PS. 23:1–6

What a powerful six verses! In the previous chapters, we have been camping out among the breathtakingly, powerful landscape these verses are painting. The word pictures here are unparalleled.

Remember the man who penned these six verses. Remember that the shepherd turned psalmist turned king wrote this poetry. These verses are meant to be confessed and sung as a song of victory. It is a poetic turn that was written to be put to music and sung from the depths of the gut to the God of the universe in His presence. It is a confession and declaration about Him and unto Him, written by a man whose eyes had seen much mileage and whose life had traversed the roads he was writing about. David had lived through the best and the worst, and through it all, he had found that his God—Yahweh his Shepherd—was faithful.

These are not the musings of a young buck who had hope but no experience. Rather it was written by a man who had the full experience and had still retained that hope. He is a man whose gray hair, rugged beard, and furrowed lines on his face alluded to a life that would be talked about long after he drew his legs onto the bed and took his last breath on this side of his journey. David could take the stand and testify as an expert in any court of law. He knew what he was talking about. And because of this, we can trust these words and allow them to be burned onto the tablet of our hearts.

We have walked through the first three verses thus far. The Lord, the I AM, the self-existent One, the God of the ages, the Almighty Ancient of Days who started this thing and will finish it as well—Yahweh—He is our Shepherd. And because of who He is, I shall not want. As long as He is my Shepherd, the God who knows my needs will meet my every need.

He makes me lie down in green pastures and leads me beside peaceful streams. He meets my physical and temporal needs, and He also meets my emotional and spiritual needs. He is the God who knows all of me and takes care of all of me—*all*. He doesn't do anything halfheartedly or halfway. He is the God who restores my soul and leads me in the right places and paths so my life will bring honor to the One who is my Shepherd. He does all of this because of His name's sake. He can do nothing less, for even if the world around us is faithless, God will be faithful because that is who He is. He can be no less and do no less than what He is. And He . . . is . . . good!

Now let's take the time to drink deeply from verse 4. Let's pause to read it again and ponder its promises. There is much to lean in and drink from.

Yea, though I walk through the valley of the shadow of death,
I will fear no evil;
For You are with me;
Your rod and Your staff, they comfort me.

—PS. 23:4

The scenery has now changed.

At first reading, we see a shift taking place. In the first three verses, we read of God as our Shepherd. He is the God who meets our needs. He leads me to green pastures and still waters and makes me lie down there if I won't do it myself. The imagery in the first three verses seems sunny, warm, and deeply tranquil. But now, the darkness of the night is creeping in. I can now smell the dampness of dusk and the coldness that comes when the sun hides its rays from the firmament I have my feet on. And as I walk, shadows are starting to abound.

This is not a place I want to be. It brings uncertainty and makes me vulnerable. I am not in control in this place. I do not like it here. It is not comfortable in any sense of the word. My bones begin to chill, and if I am honest, I can even feel my spine get a little jittery. My hairs are standing up, and my teeth are clenched. I don't like walking where I can't see. I don't like the feeling of shivering when the coldness pierces through my outer garments and begins to chill my core.

So as I immerse myself in this imagery, I see a change of scenery because time has continued to pass and my location has changed as the hours have ticked by.

The valley . . .

The psalmist is talking about a place he is walking through that is not a good place. It is a valley. The word *valley* is translated from the Hebrew word *gay* (pronounced gah'ee).[8] I found this to mean a place that gives the picture of a deep valley or, more accurately, a very narrow, dark, wet gorge with lofty sides to the left and right. Once I am in this place, there are only two ways I can move—backward or forward. I cannot go to my right or left.

In this place, I am thus much more vulnerable than before. I have little defense. My ability to protect myself is greatly diminished. My only source of light is taking flight as well. The sun has set, and the night is upon me. I cannot see the top of the steep cliffs to my left and my right, nor can I see beyond a few feet ahead of me. I cannot see the light at the end of this tunnel. I do not know what awaits me around the next turn or bend. I am greatly tempted now to turn back, but I somehow know I have to go forward. My future is ahead of me, not behind me. I must forge ahead. But the alarms in my head are ringing louder than the bells on a $5 alarm clock at wake-up time. Have I mentioned I don't like being here, that I am uncomfortable here?

If the valley is not enough, the imagery gets even more ominous.

The valley of the shadow of death . . .

This valley isn't just any valley. It is a particular valley. The valley has a name, and I really don't like it. It is the Valley of the Shadow of Death.

---

8. James Strong, *Strong's Talking Greek and Hebrew Dictionary* (WORDsearch, 2020) (Strong's 1516), WORDsearch Bible Library Electronic Database, accessed December 15, 2022.

So now, because my light is decreasing, the shadows are increasing. The darkness is getting darker, and my vision is playing tricks on me. I am not sure what I am seeing. My fear is thus starting to rise. This is a valley of the shadow, and if that isn't enough, there are two more words. It isn't just a valley. It isn't just the valley of the shadow. It is the valley of the shadow *of death*. The implication is that this is a place where I may not make it out. My journey might end here. Maybe I can't see the end of the valley because this valley is my end. After all, isn't death final?

The phrase *shadow of death* in Hebrew comes from the word *salmwet* (pronounced tsal-maw'-veth). It is two Hebrew words put together: *sel* (pronounced tsale) and *mawet* (pronounced maw'-veth).[9] This word means the "shade of death," the overshadowing of death, and the grave.[10] In South Alabama, we say this ain't good.

My heart is now pumping faster than a squirrel on an IV drip of Red Bull. I can feel every heartbeat in my chest. I begin to feel the cold sweat of fear. I can feel dread creeping up my legs, and it is trying to take every bit of strength I have left in me. I am uncomfortable and awkward. I really don't like this feeling or this place. I bet you don't either.

Here's what I noticed. This place is the psalmist's metaphor for two places.

1. *Life's gravest situations and circumstances.* It can be any situation or circumstance where the stakes are high and the loss is incalculable. It is a serious place, a tumultuous turn, a place you didn't plan to be in and now you are unsure how to navigate out of it.

The bottom line is that this valley has serious implications. We aren't playing for tiddlywinks here. This is big stuff, the stuff that could make or break you. And in this valley, this dark, wet place that is steep on

9. Ibid. (Strong's 6757), accessed December 15, 2022.
10. Ibid. (Strong's 6757), accessed December 15, 2022.

two sides and I can't see around the bend, I am vulnerable and don't know how things are going to turn out.

2. *The place of death itself.* It isn't called the valley of the shadow of death for nothing. This place is the final curtain call. It is the place that so many fear. It is the great equalizer of the prince and the pauper. No amount of money can buy your way out of this place when your appointment is so determined.

Death comes for all, and that's not for a lack of trying to avoid it. Many have tried to escape its sentence. Ponce de Leon tried to find a fountain that would foil it. It has been said that baseball great Ted Williams hoped to one day escape his sentence through a high-tech cryogenic freezer. They aren't the only ones. Tales have been told of those who have tried to buy their way out, scheme their way out, or find some secret formula to keep it from coming for them—all to no avail. Death still called. It is a place of finality. The best schemer can't cheat it. No mortal can escape its grasp.

So now we must look again at verse 4. We have been focusing on the imagery that presents the grave problem (pardon the pun). Now we need to focus on the rest.

Notice a change in pronouns. You English majors may have already noticed this, but the rest of us need to see something important. The first three verses use the pronouns He and His. They are powerful for sure. They are confessions and declarations *about* the Good Shepherd. Now the pronoun changes to *You* and stays that way for the rest of the psalm. We have gone from He and His to You and Your.

David is no longer speaking and making declarations about his Shepherd. Now he is speaking *to* his Shepherd. He is making declarations to Him of what He is now in the present tense doing for him.

The Great Shepherd is no longer leading me in the green pastures and peaceful streams. Now, when the road is treacherous and the darkness is dimming my ability to see, when I can feel the enemies' eyes glaring at me even though I can't see them, the Shepherd has moved not only near me but beside me. I can feel Him even closer now. I was in His presence before, but now His presence is very near. I can reach out and touch Him. He is with me. His presence is by me, with me, and around me. It now seems like He has encompassed me on all sides. He has my blind side. I may be walking through this valley, but I now realize I am not traveling alone.

He is with me on this journey *through* the valley . . .

I am now noticing some things I didn't see before. The psalm says I am walking through the valley of the shadow of death. I begin to understand that this isn't a place where I have to live. This is not my residence; it is not my dwelling place or my final resting spot. I am journeying *through* this place. That doesn't change the fact that I am here now, but God said I am walking through it. That means my journey doesn't end here.

Did you get that? Really?

This valley, this valley of the shadow, this valley of the shadow of death is not my final resting place. I am not General Custer, and this ain't the Battle of Little Bighorn. My story doesn't end here. God said I am going through this place. It has a starting place, and because He is with me, I can keep walking with Him and He will bring me through every twist and turn in this dark valley. Eventually, I will walk out the same way I walked in—one blessed, sure-footed step at a time. I will get through this. I will!

Readers, say it with me! Say it out loud. Your soul needs to hear your voice. So does your enemy. *I will move through this valley! My story has not been fully written yet. I have more pages in my book, and the Grand Author has more ink in His precious and potent pen.*

Didn't it feel good to say that?

And because He is with me, my focus is changing. I can tell because I am talking to Him. And I now find His presence is changing my emotional condition. His perfect love that I now feel is casting out the fear that was trying to take me over.

> *There is no fear in love; but perfect love casts out fear, because fear involves torment. But he who fears has not been made perfect in love.*
>
> —1 JOHN 4:18

I know now He is with me because I can feel Him with me. And because His presence is upon me, His love is driving the fear away. Fear can't stay where He is. My terror is running! My dread is now dreading my Shepherd. The darkness doesn't seem scary now.

> *Even there Your hand shall lead me,*
> *And Your right hand shall hold me.*
> *If I say, "Surely the darkness shall fall on me,"*
> *Even the night shall be light about me;*
> *Indeed, the darkness shall not hide from You,*
> *But the night shines as the day;*
> *The darkness and the light* are *both alike* to You.
>
> —PS. 139:10–12

I can feel Him. He is with me. His mighty right hand is holding me. And even though the darkness has fallen upon me, the night is not dark anymore. The night is illuminated by His presence. Darkness is nothing to the One whose presence drives away all shadows. He is with me. He has promised me that He will not leave me. He does not break His promises. He is the God who cannot lie.

Look at some more of God's promises to you.

> *Have I not commanded you? Be strong and of good courage; do not be afraid, nor be dismayed, for the Lord your God is with you wherever you go.*
>
> —JOSH. 1:9

But now, thus says the Lord, who created you, O Jacob,
And He who formed you, O Israel:
"Fear not, for I have redeemed you;
I have called you by your name;
You are Mine.
When you pass through the waters, I will be with you;
And through the rivers, they shall not overflow you.
When you walk through the fire, you shall not be burned,
Nor shall the flame scorch you."

—ISA. 43:1–2

And the Lord, He is the one who goes before you. He will be with you, He will not leave you nor forsake you; do not fear nor be dismayed.

—DEUT. 31:8

I sought the Lord, and He heard me,
And delivered me from all my fears.

—PS. 34:4

For God has not given us a spirit of fear, but of power and of love and of a sound mind.

—2 TIM. 1:7

For I am persuaded that neither death nor life, nor angels nor principalities nor powers, nor things present nor things to come, nor height nor depth, nor any other created thing, shall be able to separate us from the love of God which is in Christ Jesus our Lord.

—ROM. 8:38–39

For you did not receive a spirit that makes you a slave again to fear, but you received the Spirit of sonship. And by him we cry, "Abba, Father." The Spirit himself testifies with our spirit that we are God's children. Now if we are children, then we are heirs—heirs of God and co-heirs with Christ, if indeed we share in his sufferings in order that we may also share in his glory.

—ROM. 8:15–17 (NIV)

If there is one thing I can count on, friends, that one thing is Him. He said He would be with me. So I must—and you must too—stand on His promises. Come hell or high water, through fire or flood, He is with me, and He is with you too.

He is the God who not only goes with me if I stay with Him and trust in His good name, but He will fight for me.

He is the Shepherd who fights for me.

Let's look at the second part of verse 4.

> For You are *with me; Your rod and Your staff, they comfort me.*
>
> —PS. 23:4

The rod and the staff are the tools of the shepherd. They are also known as the club and the crook.

- The club (rod) is a powerful weapon the shepherd wields to protect and defend his sheep.
- The crook (staff) is another powerful tool the shepherd uses to rescue and guide his sheep.

Together, these tools help defeat the enemy and keep the sheep from going on the wrong path or falling into deep pits. They are more than enough to protect the sheep. They are more than enough to set the enemy to flight.

God is the Great and Good Shepherd who fights for me. He fights my battles. Throughout Scripture, I am reminded of God's promises to His people in this regard.

> *And Moses said to the people, "Do not be afraid. Stand still, and see the salvation of the Lord, which He will accomplish for you today. For the*

Egyptians whom you see today, you shall see again no more forever. The Lord will fight for you, and you shall hold your peace."

—EXOD. 14:13–14

You will not need to fight in this battle. Position yourselves, stand still and see the salvation of the Lord, who is with you, O Judah and Jerusalem! Do not fear or be dismayed; tomorrow go out against them, for the Lord is with you.

—2 CHRON. 20:17

One of you routs a thousand, because the LORD your God fights for you, just as he promised.

—JOSH. 23:10 (NIV)

"No weapon formed against you shall prosper,
And every tongue which *rises against you in judgment*
You shall condemn.
This is *the heritage of the servants of the Lord,*
And their righteousness is from Me,"
Says the Lord.

—ISA. 54:17

The valley of the shadow of death in proper perspective . . .

And now I look at this valley differently. I feel differently. I see differently. I feel Your presence, Lord. I see Your club and Your crook, Your rod, and Your staff. I am comforted by them, and I now feel secure. I stand up and walk tall. I am not afraid. Fear has been driven out. And now I see something else.

This valley I am traveling through is called the Shadow of Death. Remember the Hebrew word that was made from two Hebrew words? Thus, it is not called the Valley of Death. It isn't the place where I am finished. I am not done there. Rather it is called the Valley of the *Shadow* of Death. And now I begin meditating on what a shadow really is.

A shadow is evidence of something that is getting close to me. The object is overshadowing me, and light is diminished because of it. It is thus darker in a shadow for sure, but the shadow is just that—a shadow. It is *not* the actual thing. It seems that way because the object is a little closer. The object is putting a shadow on me, but the object has not touched me. Only the shadow is upon me.

Then I really started to understand. At that moment, the Holy Spirit reminded me of what God sent His Son to do for me. David was prophesying it. Now it has been done. This valley is the shadow of death because Jesus defeated it! He became the firstfruits.

> *But now Christ is risen from the dead, and has become the firstfruits of those who have fallen asleep. For since by man came death, by Man also came the resurrection of the dead. For as in Adam all die, even so in Christ all shall be made alive.*
>
> —1 COR. 15:20–22

> *For this corruptible must put on incorruption, and this mortal must put on immortality. So when this corruptible has put on incorruption, and this mortal has put on immortality, then shall be brought to pass the saying that is written: "Death is swallowed up in victory." "O Death, where is your sting? O Hades, where is your victory?" The sting of death is sin, and the strength of sin is the law. But thanks be to God, who gives us the victory through our Lord Jesus Christ. Therefore, my beloved brethren, be steadfast, immovable, always abounding in the work of the Lord, knowing that your labor is not in vain in the Lord.*
>
> —1 COR. 15:53–58

Jesus defeated death! Through Christ, death no longer has a sting.

No matter what situation I am facing, it is just a shadow. Jesus the Good Shepherd has won! He has defeated the enemy at his own game, the enemy who no longer has the keys to death, hell, and the grave. *My Jesus does!* No valley, not even death, scares me anymore. Why? Because death for those who have made the Lord Jesus their Shepherd is not final for them. It is just a transition into God's eternal, life-giving presence.

> *We are confident, yes, well pleased rather to be absent from the body and to be present with the Lord.*
>
>   —2 COR. 5:8

Even death is not the end. Fear no longer has a grip on me if I won't let it. Its authority has been broken, and I have been given the authority to conquer it by the One who sealed my victory. Jesus is the King of kings! He defeated the great equalizer. He did what Ponce de Leon could not do. Jesus defeated the finality of death. Even death cannot stop me. I am His now. I am His tomorrow. I am His the next day. And when the death bell tolls for me, I am still His. I have just changed addresses. You can find me at 123 Heavenly Lane, Jesusville, Heaven—with Him. He is the resurrection and the life. Even though we might die, we shall then really live.

No grave situation is the end for me. The Lord is my Shepherd. I am walking through the valley, but it sure ain't the end. I am traveling through it. I know He is with me. I shall fear no evil, for He has driven fear out of my heart because I have given my heart to Him, and the two can't live together. He is with me. His rod and staff make me feel secure. I am not in the valley of death. I am walking through the valley of the shadow. It is not final because the One who defeated death is right with me.

And I am even feasting in His presence at a table He has made for me in the presence of my enemies. We'll look at that in the next chapter.

Glory to the God who is with us! Even though we may walk *through* the valley of the *shadow* of death, we shall fear no evil, for Your rod and Your staff comfort us.

We will be just fine because our Shepherd has now come by our side. And He finishes what He starts (Phil. 1:6).

Notes

Chapter Five

The Shepherd Prepares a Table

What a powerful journey we have been on. Let's review this psalm again. Every time we read it, we are embedding it deep without our hearts.

The Lord is my shepherd;
I shall not want.
He makes me to lie down in green pastures;
He leads me beside the still waters.
He restores my soul;
He leads me in the paths of righteousness
For His name's sake.

Yea, though I walk through the valley of the shadow of death,
I will fear no evil;
For You are with me;
Your rod and Your staff, they comfort me.

You prepare a table before me in the presence of my enemies;
You anoint my head with oil;
My cup runs over.
Surely goodness and mercy shall follow me
All the days of my life;
And I will dwell in the house of the Lord
Forever.

—PS. 23:1–6

Up to this point we have walked through the first four verses of Psalm 23. Remember that this psalm is first a declaration and a confession. It is a declaration that God—the Lord of heaven and of earth, the I AM, the self-existent One, the Ancient of Days who created all that we see and even what we don't, Yahweh—He is my Shepherd. He is the One who leads me, guides me, provides for me, and protects me. It is further a declaration that I have made to Yahweh, my Shepherd. He is my God. This is a personal thing. And for this to work, I need to confess God as my God.

For these promises to be made mine, for me to seize them and stand in quiet trust upon them, God must be my God. This God, my God, keeps me from lack. He is out front leading me to a place of green pastures and still waters. It is a place of provision and peace. My needs are being met both physically and spiritually. Not only is He bringing my body to a place of provision and rest, but this Great and Good Shepherd is leading my soul to refreshment and restoration. He is leading me in right paths. So as long as I have made Him my Shepherd and follow His lead, I will walk the right paths. These paths will bring honor to His name and purpose to mine.

As God was leading, we found that the scenery changed. The day began turning to night, and my situation became grave. I began walking into a valley, and not just any valley but the Valley of the Shadow of Death. It was a particular place called by a particular name. It was a name that indicated finality. I couldn't see the way out and thought I might not make it through this place. But the Shepherd who was out front—when the night and fog drifted in upon me and the coldness began to penetrate my bones—I felt a very real presence beside me. The Shepherd who had been out front was now beside me. And as this happened, His presence reassured me, and the fear that was paralyzing me began to leave. I was comforted and felt security from His rod and His staff.

Now we are at verse 5. Let's read it together and soak in its words.

You prepare a table before me in the presence of my enemies;
You anoint my head with oil;
My cup runs over.

—PS. 23:5

David is speaking from experience in verse 5. As I read this, I again remembered the man who penned these words. David had experienced the words he had written.

David had been a man on the run. He had been chased from his home and his life by people who had turned on him, declared him to be an enemy, and tried to run him down and put him down like a haggard, rabid dog. As he is writing these words, I believe he has to be remembering times in the past.

Running from Saul (1 Sam. 21:6)

One such time when David was on the run was when he had to flee in great haste because King Saul wanted to kill him. Saul had placed a hit order on David's head. David had to flee quickly and thus had no weapons to protect him and no food to sustain him. He came to the place of God's Tabernacle which was set up in a village called Nob. David was given the very showbread that had been in the presence of the Lord and was reserved for the priests. God sustained him in the presence of his enemies. God showed Himself faithful when David desperately needed a good hand upon him.

Spurned by Nabal (1 Sam. 25:18)

But that wasn't the only time. David was out in the cold, living as an outlaw for some time. He was particularly low this time. Samuel, the man who had anointed him, had died, and David's hope was running low because of it. Would he die? Would God's word to him not come to pass? He was living between the times—the time between the promise and the palace. He is now living in the trenches of the process. It was a time of transition, the time between what God said would come to pass and the time it actually came to fruition. The time between was a grind. God's promises seemed so far away. David was living as an outlaw, but now men had come to reside in the caves with him. They were mighty men who needed leadership from a man who knew how to run to and trust his Shepherd.

Now responsible for more people than himself, David found that their food had nearly run out and they were in great need of provisions. He thought he would find help from a man named Nabal whose servants he had protected some time back, but his request was spurned with disgust. Wounded and already running low on hope, David wanted to give it all up and lash out in anger and frustration. In this low moment when he felt surrounded by the enemy on all sides, a woman named Abigail, whose name means "the father's joy," showed David the love and wisdom of God the Father.[11] She loaded donkeys with bread, wine, roasted grain, and figs. She even gave David lamb to feast on. She provided David with the provision of the Lord at just the right time. This mighty woman not only provided a table of provision for David and his men but reminded David of who he was and of God's calling on his life. David was living in process, but it was all part of a process that was training him for reigning. He was learning how to reign as a king through the anointing and direction of the King of all kings.

And that wouldn't be the last time.

Running from Absalom (2 Sam. 17:27–29)

Even after becoming king, David would have to fight many battles and run for his life again. This time it was from Absalom, his own son. Absalom had set himself up as king, usurped the throne, and sought to snuff out his father's candle. And David went on the run again. His

11. Roswell D. Hitchcock, *Hitchcock's Bible Names Dictionary*, WORDsearch Bible Library Electronic Database, accessed December 15, 2022.

enemies wanted him gone, but God provided David with a table of wheat, barley, flour, grain, honey, curds, and cheese.

David had tables prepared for him in the presence of his enemies. He knew what he was talking about. Here in the 23rd Psalm, David is giving us a picture of God's presence, His provision, and His protection during great battles, resistance, and turmoil.

You prepare a table before me in the presence of my enemies.

Let's look closely at this verse and ponder the words.

Prepare

The word *prepare* comes from a Hebrew word that means "to set in order."[12] So when the enemy has surrounded you and you have made the Lord your Shepherd, God will *arak* (pronounced aw-rak'). He will arrange things. He will set the battle in a certain order. He will join the battle and set His plan in motion.

In doing this, He prepares a table—but not just any table.

Table

The Hebrew word for table is not just any table. It is *shulhan* (pronounced shool-khawn'), a spread-out table.[13] It is a big table with a large spread-out meal on it.

This table is set before me. It means that it is put before me, in front of me. I have been given a seat, and that table is set right in front of me. I am sitting in the seat of honor.

---

12. James Strong, *Strong's Talking Greek and Hebrew Dictionary* (WORDsearch, 2020) (Strong's 6186), WORDsearch Bible Library Electronic Database, accessed December 15, 2022.

13. Ibid. (Strong's 7979), accessed December 15, 2022.

In the presence of my enemies

This table that has been set in order before me is not just set up in any place. It is set before me in the presence of my enemies. That means the enemy, or *sarar* (pronounced tsaw-rar') that is trying to distress me, bind me up and afflict me is besieging me on all sides and trying to trouble me and even destroy me.[14] This enemy has to stop his advance.

This table is set in order in front of me in the presence of my enemies. The enemy cannot touch me in this place. He can only glare and watch me while I am in this place at the table.

My head is anointed with oil

I am not sure about the order of this. It seems the table is set and prepared and I am seated first. But it might be that my head is anointed with oil and then I get to sit with this table in front of me.

In any case, I found some interesting things about this anointing.

The first thing is that a shepherd anoints his sheep with oil at times, especially when they are wounded. I found this was for three reasons.[15]

1. The shepherd anoints his sheep with oil to soothe and heal their wounds.

2. The shepherd anoints his sheep with oil to repel insects, especially the ones that bite and pester them, bringing pain and great distraction when the shepherd is trying to lead them to the right places.

---

14. Ibid. (Strong's 6887), accessed December 15, 2022.

15. Paraphrased from *The Preacher's Outline & Sermon Bible (POSB)* (Chattanooga: Leadership Ministries Worldwide), Copyright 1991, 1996, 2004 by Alpha-Omega Ministries, Inc., WORD-search Bible Library Electronic Database, accessed December 15, 2022, (Psalm 23 Commentary).

3. The shepherd anoints his sheep with oil because the fragrance of the anointing repelled snakes that would sometimes hide nearby in the tall grass.

I am sure David is reflecting on the anointing he provided his sheep as a young shepherd.

I can't also help but think that David is reflecting on the time the Prophet Samuel anointed him years before.

I took a class some years ago from the professor, Bible scholar, and author Dr. Ronald E. Cottle. In his course "The Anointing: Its Nature and How to Receive It," he taught me some things about anointing that are important and applicable to our journey here.

The oil of anointing was called *shemen* (pronounced she'-men) in Hebrew. It is a reference to the oil used for a particular purpose. God told the priests to prepare anointing oil to use in a very particular and set way (Exod. 30:22–25).

The priests set aside 5 quarts of olive oil (*shemen*) and then added four ingredients—14 pounds of myrrh, 7 pounds of sweet cinnamon, 7 pounds of calamus, and 14 pounds of cassia. Mixing them into the 5 quarts of olive oil resulted in a heavy oil with a very distinctive smell. The ingredients added to the oil gave it some healing qualities. Dr. Cottle said this oil was called the *Shemen-Ya*—the oil of God.[16]

It was an anointing that symbolized the life of God released into the one who was anointed. When the oil of anointing was used to anoint (Hebrew: *mesach*) a person, the anointed became an anointed one (Hebrew: *mashiach*). This person was given enablement—ability and authority by the God of the universe. Interestingly, the word *shemen* is also translated semen, which we know as the reproductive seed of a

16. Dr. Ronald E. Cottle, "The Anointing: Its Nature and How to Receive It" (college course, Christian Life School of Theology Global. Columbus, GA).

man. This reproductive seed has the man's DNA in it. His life essence is in his reproductive seed.[17]

The *shemen* anointing of God thus carries the reproductive essence of God. His enablement ability and authority to reproduce and do what He purposed was set upon the one being anointed.

The Word of God tells us that the *Shemen-Ya* was poured on David's head, and when that occurred, the Spirit of God came upon him from that day forward (1 Sam. 16:12–13). From that moment, God saw David as king even though men did not yet acknowledge what God had conferred. But everyone around David knew there was something different and powerful about him.

David had to have remembered that day—the day God pulled him out of the sheep fields and anointed him among a bunch of jealous brothers who thought little of him. But God saw what all others had overlooked.

David was reflecting on the God who would take care of him amid great conflict and cause his cup to run over no matter what schemes the enemy had hatched. God would also provide an anointing of enablement—power and authority to accomplish all God had called him to. He is the God who is more than enough.

My mind's eye vision

As I was studying and praying about this passage, a vision began to unfold in my mind, and I began writing it down.

Here is what I saw.

During my battle—my serious battle, even in the Valley of the Shadow of Death when my situation is grave—I remember that You are with

---

17. Ibid.

me, and thus I shall not fear. Your rod and Your staff bring me comfort and security. And then I find that during this battle when the enemy has surrounded me on all sides when it seems like all hope is lost, my Shepherd stems the tide. The Shepherd who was out in front of me is now beside me, and with one rise of His hand, the enemy's advance is halted and stymied.

As I am standing there, my Shepherd turns to me, opens up a container, and anoints my head with oil. He puts it on my head. It runs down my face and continues to the edge of my garments (Ps. 133:2).

It is thus an anointing that covers me. It is thick and has a very distinctive fragrance. As I feel it applied and as it slowly runs down my body, I feel the wounds I have sustained in battle begin to soothe. The throbbing pain I was feeling begins to subside, and my bleeding stops. My open wounds begin to close. This anointing is a miraculous salve that is salvific in nature. As I am in awe of what is happening to me, I notice that the thoughts of dismay and the shouts of my demise that had been ringing in my ears and hindering my progress, biting at me like pesky insects on my flesh, cease. I just hear silence now. It is almost deafening. In this place, I now notice something even more dramatic. The scene nearly takes my breath away. I stand in awe and silence.

The fragrance of my anointing reaches the nostrils of my enemies who immediately recognize its distinct aroma and not only stop their posture of advance but take three steps back. This evil horde sent to do me in now begins giving me room. I am still surrounded, but the enemies are repulsed by this aroma of anointing and are giving me room. They are furious about this development, screaming and cursing about it, but it doesn't bother me at all. All I can feel is the heavy weight of the anointing upon me and the Shepherd who is with me.

And then the Shepherd gives a command.

Out of His mouth erupts a thunderous voice that sounds something like mighty rivers rushing, and at the Shepherd's voice, all other voices grow silent. Upon the utterance of the command, heaven above me opens, and an object like a great sheet bound at the four corners descends in front of me. As this happens, a great banquet table appears before me, and this sheet is placed carefully on the table. I now see what is on the sheet—a great banquet feast of the best food and the choicest morsels I have ever seen. It is a feast of feasts! It is all placed before me. Then a chair appears, and the Shepherd invites me to sit in this place of honor (Acts 10:13; Rev. 19:6–9).

As I sit at this feast and draw my chair up to the table prepared before me, the enemy howls and takes another step back. Darkness is around me, but the light from an opened heaven is upon me. It illuminates my position, and the glow of the smears of the anointing reflects off of me. The fragrance of it is all around me.

As the enemy glares and watches this scene, the Shepherd invites me to eat. The enemy is watching my every move. His minions' weapons are still formed against me and burnished, but I realize they cannot make one step of advancement toward me. As I take my first bite, they take another step back. More room is made for me.

My Shepherd sits beside me, inviting me to partake. I eat to the full. I am completely satisfied.

Then I see something else on the table. In the center of this very large table are two items—a plate of bread and a pitcher of wine.

My Shepherd reaches out, breaks off a piece of this bread, and places the broken piece in my hand. In my other hand, He places a beautiful gleaming cup and then pours wine into it from the pitcher. The wine is filling my cup. He keeps pouring until the cup overflows and pours on the table and even spills out onto me. It runs down my arm, and as it does, it feels like it is covering me—almost like the anointing oil did earlier. It is a strange sensation, but it doesn't bother me. In fact, it gives me an overwhelming feeling of peace. All my enemies are bothered by it. When they saw the wine being poured out, they howled in terror.

They stepped back even more. And when that precious liquid over-flowed, it purified everything it touched. When it hit the table, the table became so white that its brilliance caused me to squint in its radiance.

I was full before from the meal I had just eaten, but as the bread and wine were placed in my hands, I felt a longing arise deep within me for both. I felt a hunger arise in me for this bread, and my feeling of thirst for this wine was the deepest of yearnings I have ever known.

The Shepherd then invited me to partake of the bread and the wine. He did this by saying, "Take. Eat. This is My body which is broken for you. Take and drink. This cup is the new covenant in My blood" (1 Cor. 11:23).

I eat and feel warmth enter me. I drink, and not only is my deepest thirst quenched but my soul is satisfied as well (John 6:35, 48, 50–51, 53–58).

I understand now that I am taking in the body and the blood of Jesus. The Shepherd who was by me is now in me. When I drank it, the effect it had on the table happened to me. My clothing became as white as snow. My robe was so white that it shined all about me.

This became too much for the enemy. The anointing upon me, the Bread of Life now part of me, and the precious blood now covering me made the enemy cower in fear and then flee in terror. When I stood up and looked, I saw that the enemy was no longer present. They no longer pursued me. There was only my Shepherd's presence. Only my Savior was there with me.

But now my Shepherd looked different. His hair was as white as wool, even whiter than snow. His feet were like fine brass as though refined in a furnace, and His voice was like the sound of many rushing waters. He was called Faithful and True, and in righteousness He judges and makes war. His eyes were like a flame of fire, and on His head were many crowns. He had a name written that no one knew except Him.

He was clothed with a robe dipped in blood, and His name was the Word of God (Rev. 1:13–15; 19:11–13).

My Shepherd didn't look like a shepherd anymore.

He is the Alpha and Omega, the First and the Last, the Lion of the Tribe of Judah, the Lamb slain for our sins from the foundation of the world who on the third day rose again, forever sealing our victory. He is now the King of kings and Lord of lords. And this King was there in front of me! I bowed before Him in worship. My enemy was defeated, and I was forever saved.

Indeed, my cup was running over.

Then the vision ended.

Friends, this vision is the picture of the Shepherd who prepares a table before you in the presence of your enemies. He will anoint you with the Shemen-Ya—the distinctive oil of God giving you the enablement of the Holy Spirit in both authority and power. And with the Word of God—the Bread of Life—as the testimony on your lips and the blood of the Lamb appropriated upon you, you will defeat the enemy (Rev. 12:11). *No* weapon formed against you shall prosper.

> "*No weapon formed against you shall prosper,*
> *And every tongue which rises against you in judgment*
> *You shall condemn.*
> *This is the heritage of the servants of the Lord,*
> *And their righteousness is from Me,*"
> *Says the Lord.*
>
> —ISA. 54:17

Praise God for the Great and Good Shepherd! He has prepared a table before us in the presence of our enemy. He has anointed our heads with oil. Our cup truly runs over.

Praise the God who fights for me!

He is the same God who fights for you!

Notes

Chapter Six

The Good Shepherd Who Is Good Through It All

What amazing power rests in these six verses! What a journey we have taken as we have camped in the imagery of these life-altering words. We have read this psalm together for five chapters. Now I want you to take a minute and thank God for what He has shown you so far. As we begin this chapter, take a moment to worship Him for a minute or two.

Now together just one more time, let's read this psalm.

The Lord is my shepherd;
I shall not want.
He makes me to lie down in green pastures;
He leads me beside the still waters.
He restores my soul;
He leads me in the paths of righteousness
For His name's sake.

Yea, though I walk through the valley of the shadow of death,
I will fear no evil;
For You are with me;
Your rod and Your staff, they comfort me.

You prepare a table before me in the presence of my enemies;
You anoint my head with oil;
My cup runs over.
Surely goodness and mercy shall follow me
All the days of my life;

And I will dwell in the house of the Lord
Forever.

—PS. 23:1–6

In this chapter, we will complete our walk through the 23rd Psalm. We will focus on the last verse. Let's look at this verse in the Amplified Version before we go forward. It will help you as we unpack it together.

Surely or only goodness, mercy, and unfailing love shall follow me all the days of my life, and through the length of my days the house of the Lord [and His presence] shall be my dwelling place.

—PS. 23:6 (AMPC)

In this verse, I believe David is completing his look back on his life. His reflections are all coming together in a grand crescendo. All the events, happenings, circumstances, and situations he had been in, walked through, and endured are passing through his mind like a grand movie flashing from frame to frame.

David remembers, he knows, and he wants every reader who picks up this song to fully understand just how faithful his Shepherd has been to him. He is reminded of God's constant and consistent care and love. So, he starts with the word *surely*.

Surely . . .

This is not a word of probability. It is not wishful thinking, and it is not a hope-filled feeling. For David, this word is a life marker. It is a word he placed in this last sentence to help us understand that this place is a place of certainty. It is a certain thing. It is the bedrock and true. It can be stood upon in quiet trust as something no wind can blow down and no flood can wash away. It is as sure as the air he is breathing in his lungs, as the sun shining on his face. The words that come next are sure. You can count on them. They are a promise not just from David but from our Heavenly Father. Count on them. God doesn't break His word. He can't lie. *Surely* . . . God's goodness and mercy are following us.

But what does that mean? Let's seek to understand.

Goodness

The word *goodness* is translated from the Hebrew word *towb* (pronounced tobe).[18] It means good, well, favorable, festive, pleasant, pleasing, better, right, even best.[19] It is a word that is meant to communicate the concept of good in every sense of the word.

It means that the Great Shepherd—the God of the universe—*is good.* He is the God whose love for us cannot be quenched. His thoughts for us cannot be counted. His plans for us take our breath away. And the inheritance He has laid aside for us cannot be fully quantified. Your God is good. He loves you. He delights in the thought of you.

And in a world that is full of fractious hate and communicates a version of love that leaves us lacking and cold, we need to hear and understand this message. Your God—the God of the universe who set this world in order—made you. You are His masterpiece, and He delights in you.

As I write this, I am reminded of the Word of the Lord to us in Zephaniah. It is a powerful passage that fits here.

> *The Lord your God in your midst,*
> *The Mighty One, will save;*
> *He will rejoice over you with gladness,*
> *He will quiet you with His love,*
> *He will rejoice over you with singing.*

—ZEPH. 3:17

God is the God who wants nothing to separate us from His love and His presence. After all, that is why Jesus came—to eradicate the separation

---

18. James Strong, *Strong's Talking Greek and Hebrew Dictionary* (WORDsearch, 2020) (Strong's 2896), WORDsearch Bible Library Electronic Database, accessed December 15, 2022.
19. Ibid. (Strong's 2896), Also-W.E. Vine, Vine's *Complete Expository Dictionary of the Old and New Testament* (Nashville, Thomas Nelson Publishers), WORDsearch Bible Library Electronic Database (WORDsearch, 2004), accessed December 15, 2022.

that existed between God and mankind because of sin. He is the God who wants you to reside in His presence. He is the Mighty One who saves. And this God rejoices over you with gladness and singing. He quiets you with His love. This is a delightful picture to me.

I believe David is trying to convey to us that God has proven throughout his life to be *good* in every sense of the word, even through every up and down. God has been and continues to be good.

Now let's look at the next word.

Mercy

The word *mercy* is translated from the Hebrew word *hesed* (pronounced khe'-sed).[20] It can mean mercy, kindness, favor, and loving-kindness.[21] It can also mean steadfast love, grace, faithfulness, goodness, and devotion.[22]

As we look at these two words together—*towb* and *hesed*—the second word seems to be a deepening of the first. The two put together give us a picture of God's goodness that is deepened and further opened up to us. God is good, and His goodness includes His mercy and grace-filled loving-kindness toward us.

I am reminded of a few other psalms that are helpful to us here. Interestingly, these psalms are attributed to David as well.

> *The LORD is merciful and gracious, Slow to anger, and abounding in mercy.*
> —PS. 103:8

20. James Strong, *Strong's Talking Greek and Hebrew Dictionary* (WORDsearch, 2020) (Strong's 2617), WORDsearch Bible Library Electronic Database, accessed December 15, 2022.
21. Ibid. (Strong's 2617), accessed December 15, 2022.
22. W.E. Vine, Vine's *Complete Expository Dictionary of the Old and New Testament* (Nashville, Thomas Nelson Publishers), WORDsearch Bible Library Electronic Database (WORDsearch, 2004), (Strong's 2617), accessed December 15, 2022.

The LORD is compassionate and gracious, Slow to anger and abounding in lovingkindness.

—PS. 103:8 (NASB)

The LORD is gracious and full of compassion, Slow to anger and great in mercy.

—PS. 145:8

The Lord is gracious and full of compassion, slow to anger and abounding in mercy and loving-kindness.

—PS. 145:8 (AMPC)

For You, Lord, are good, and ready to forgive, And abundant in mercy to all those who call upon You.

—PS. 86:5

But You, O Lord, are a God full of compassion, and gracious, Longsuffering and abundant in mercy and truth.

—PS. 86:15

For the LORD is good; His mercy is everlasting, And His truth endures to all generations.

—PS. 100:5

I believe David is speaking of God—his God who is his Shepherd. His Great Shepherd is full of goodness and mercy. He is good in every sense of the word. And that goodness means He is full of mercy and grace-filled loving-kindness. It is an overflowing love that is relentless in its pursuit.

David knew his God loved him. That is why he said *surely*. It is a certainty.

I imagine David was remembering just how good God had been.

- ✓ When David was a shepherd boy in the fields facing both the lion and the bear, God had shown Himself to be good.
- ✓ When David took one of five smooth stones from his shepherd's bag, put that stone in his sling, and then charged a raging giant with the courage of a lion and a faith that took the breath away of the other soldiers who could only gape with their mouths wide open, he found God to be good.
- ✓ David slung that stone hard and true, and it sunk into the forehead of that cursing giant whose fall could be heard far across the countryside. Then David pried out of the giant's hand the very sword he had raised and threatened to kill David with and cut the giant's head off. God was good. Even at insurmountable odds, God proved to be good.
- ✓ God was still good when David was hiding in a cave like a criminal.
- ✓ God was still good when David found himself living in the territory of the enemy yet remained untouched and unharmed.

God was always good.

- ✓ God was good when David had much.
- ✓ God was good when David and his mighty men had little.
- ✓ God was the God who prepared a table before David in the presence of his enemies on more than one occasion.
- ✓ God was the good God who anointed his head with oil, who caused his cup to run over and not only fill his belly but overflow his heart with an unquenchable love and forever captivate his loyalty.
- ✓ God was good—in every sense of the word.

And then this God—David's God—had been merciful. He had shown David great compassion, loving kindness, and breathtaking mercy.

There was a season when David allowed his heart to stray from this good God. He let the cares of this life distract him. He allowed the glimmer of the earthly pleasures he was given to lull him into a place of distraction and ease. He lost his watchful eye. He forgot that the enemy never lost sight of trying to take him down. Rather than staying in the fight and strapping on his sword when kings normally go out to war (2 Sam. 11:1), David stayed behind, wandering off purpose on top of his palace, looking for something to do. He should have picked up his instrument in that place and worshiped; it would have brought his focus back. But instead, in the absence of purposed activity, the enemy of his heart provided an opportunity to fill the void. When he saw Bathsheba, he took the bait.

Adultery ensued, and in an attempt to save face and keep his sin hidden, the dark rabbit hole he had gone down got darker and deeper. His sin festered and compounded in that darkness that should have been brought to light. In this place, this once-humble shepherd boy who had been anointed as God's appointed king had a man murdered, causing others to be complicit in his horrid, senseless sin.

Punishment soon followed. God could not leave David's actions unaccounted for. And when fully confronted with the dreadfulness of his sin, David confessed all. He accepted the punishment, a penalty that was, indeed, severe. Sin's penalty always is. Its cost is truly more than we can bear.

In the stillness, David reflected. He picked up his instrument, and with pen and paper, this king repented. It was no halfhearted thing. He wrote a song about it, publicly published it, and has it sung at the place where he knew God's presence would rest. It was near the seat that he desperately needed to reach—the Mercy Seat.

The 51st Psalm is the result.

It is one of the most powerful pictures of heartfelt repentance I have ever witnessed. David acknowledged his transgressions. He confessed his iniquities and asked for cleansing for his dire and dreadful sins. In doing so, David came to a revelation. He fully found what he feared the most.

He uncovered his chief and deepest fear. It wasn't that he might lose the kingdom God had given him. It wasn't losing the riches he had amassed. It wasn't being stripped of the notoriety or fame that had come to him. It wasn't even his family. David's chief fear was losing the presence of the Holy Spirit in his life.

> *Do not cast me away from Your presence,*
> *And do not take Your Holy Spirit from me.*

—PS. 51:11

He could not bear the thought of being cast away from God's presence or having His Holy Spirit taken from him. Wow! We could learn much from this man in this one sentence.

God heard that prayer. The Merciful One reached out from that Mercy Seat and extended grace to David out of His deep and everlasting loving-kindness. And thus, through the good *and* the bad, through even his worst sin, David found God to not only be good in every sense of the word but also to be full of mercy and grace.

David knew of God's goodness and mercy. He had drunk deeply from that cup time and time again and found that it never ran dry. What's more, David was sure this goodness and mercy would not only be with him in the past and the present . . .

. . . but that it would pursue him.

We know this by David's choice of the word *follow*. It is the Hebrew word *radap* (pronounced raw-daf').[23] It is a word that means to chase after, pursue, or even run down.[24]

Thus, David seems to be saying that God's goodness and merciful loving-kindness are sure and that it chased after him. They pursued him to overtake him.

---

23. James Strong, *Strong's Talking Greek and Hebrew Dictionary* (WORDsearch, 2020) (Strong's 7291), WORDsearch Bible Library Electronic Database, accessed December 15, 2022.
24. Ibid. (Strong's 7291), accessed December 15, 2022.

Even when he felt far away from God's goodness and loving-kindness, even when he had run away from them by his own choices and sin, God was still in hot pursuit. And God's goodness and loving-kindness would pursue him all the days of his life.

> *Surely goodness and mercy shall follow me*
> *All the days of my life;*
> *And I will dwell in the house of the Lord*
> *Forever.*

—PS. 23:6

Days . . . a definite period of time

David's choice of the word *days* is translated in Hebrew as *yome*.[25] It is a word that represents a period of time.[26] It can even refer to the daytime or the daytime of his life—the days of his living, his waking, and his living breath. It can be from the time he was born until the time he breathed his last breath—every moment and every single second is covered here—all of it.

God's goodness and mercy were sure. They had pursued him, and they would continue to do so. They had run him down and found him. He had embraced them, and now he was running with them. He knew God's goodness and mercy were sure. They wouldn't leave him or forsake him. They would pursue him all the days of his life.

And in this place, David wanted to *dwell.*

A place called Dwell

---

25. Ibid. (Strong's 3117), accessed December 15, 2022.
26. W.E. Vine, Vine's *Complete Expository Dictionary of the Old and New Testament* (Nashville, Thomas Nelson Publishers), WORDsearch Bible Library Electronic Database (WORDsearch, 2004), (Strong's 3117), accessed December 15, 2022.

Now notice the word *dwell*. It is the Hebrew word *yashab* (pronounced yaw-shab').[27] It means to dwell, inhabit, remain, sit down in, and even marry.[28] Thus we see a picture of a place you stay, sit down in, and remain in that becomes a place where you dwell.

This place is called Dwell, and it is the place of God's manifest presence.

David gives us the picture of this place called Dwell as God's house. David loved God's house. He literally wanted to live there if he was able. He wrote about this desire several times.

> *I was glad when they said to me, "Let us go into the house of the Lord."*
>
> —PS. 122:1

> *One* thing *I have desired of the Lord,*
> *That will I seek:*
> *That I may dwell in the house of the Lord*
> *All the days of my life,*
> *To behold the beauty of the Lord,*
> *And to inquire in His temple.*
>
> —PS. 27:4

David had even wanted to build a permanent house for the Lord. He loved to be in God's house. It was all because of God's presence. His presence was light and life to David. He wanted to live in this place called Dwell.

And because of this love and longing, David found the secret to dwelling there—through his praise.

---

27. James Strong, *Strong's Talking Greek and Hebrew Dictionary* (WORDsearch, 2020) (Strong's 3427), WORDsearch Bible Library Electronic Database, accessed December 15, 2022.
28. Ibid. (Strong's 3427), accessed December 15, 2022.

He found that this place—this place called Dwell—was connected to a position and activity. It was the position of humble and heartfelt worship in the activity of praise.

King David was first and foremost a worshiper. He was a worshiping son who learned to pay constant honor, respect, reverence, and tribute to his good, good Father.

And that posture was the key to God's heart and crucial to maintaining his fire and passion toward his good and merciful Shepherd. This lifelong habit had carried him to this place called Dwell—the Place of God's Presence—and it would further propel him into God's eternal presence one day soon.

Forever

And thus David uses the word *forever* to go beyond his own *yome*—his days on earth—and give us a glimpse beyond his life-song on this earth.

His life would go on. God's goodness and mercy would not only pursue him in this life but would carry him much farther. David would continue to sing his songs of worship to his God long after he took his last breath on this earth and slipped beyond the veil into the eternity of God's presence in heaven when he would see with his eyes what his faith told him was there all along.

David's song would not be stifled. His story was not finished. His lungs could still belt out a new chorus. His hands would still be able to run their fingers across strings in a tribute to his Lord. But now—now—he would get to join an army chorus of angels with a melody that was so powerful that elders would cast their crowns at the feet of the Lamb who won our forever pardon. David's eyes would behold his Shepherd, and he would be there forever.

God's goodness and mercy would take him through the veil of life into real living where the presence of God is without measure.

His mouth had sung of it.

His imagination had danced at the thought of it.

His heart had longed for it.

But now as he wrote the last word of this grand opus of his life, forever.

He knew his eyes would behold his Lord.

He would soon experience what his hope had long rested on.

And what a day that would be! David would soon be part of an endless hallelujah with the inhabitants of heaven.

> *And when the Chief Shepherd appears, you will receive the crown of glory that does not fade away.*
>
> —1 PET. 5:4

What a day that had to be for David.

What a day it will be for us if we make the Chief Shepherd our Shepherd and stay faithful to His good and holy name. A crown will await us—a crown that will never tarnish or fade away.

Notes

Chapter Seven

Twenty-Three:
Your Song of Victory

The psalm is finished.

David is now finished with his song. He has written it. He looks it over. He dots every "I" and crosses every "T." He proofreads it to make sure it is what he wants to communicate.

It is. It truly is, for he heard the words whispered in his ear from the mouth of the Holy Spirit Himself. He was really not the author but rather the transcriber. So now he publishes it. They are not just words. These words are a song that is to be *sung*.

Friends, as we close our time together, we must not forget that this is a song to be sung with all our hearts—with all our might.

It is a song that is a declaration and confession of need and then a proclamation of God's provision, guidance, protection, faithfulness, goodness, and love.

It is even an atomic bomb of a weapon that when sung and proclaimed in faith makes all of hell run for cover.

Yes, it is meant to be proclaimed from the mouths of the earth worshipers who took the place of the honored cherub prince of worship who once tried to glean that worship for himself. Satan knows its power. He was flung from his place of honor and is now soon facing the eternal penalty that has already been pronounced.

The earth worshipers take this song and declare it by faith, standing on its promises, worshiping before everything has been worked out amid their valleys, in the middle of their shadows, despite their fears. They soon find that this song electrifies the atmosphere and sets the battle in order.

- ✓ Angels rush in.
- ✓ Heaven smiles.
- ✓ God sends the help He promised.
- ✓ The Holy Spirit provides an anointing of power, authority, and provision.
- ✓ And Satan knows he is done!

This, friends is a battle song. And it will propel you to victory, all the while reminding you of the Shepherd who not only leads you and goes before you but is by you and in you.

What a song! "Twenty-Three."

Say it. Sing it. Commit it to memory. Stand in quiet trust on the foundation of these words.

Its sayings are faithful. Remember that the Holy Spirit is the real author of this song.

These words are the song of your victory.

May we, too, live in this place called Dwell, the place of God's glorious presence.

And in these last days, this Tabernacle is being built again (Acts 15:16–17).

✓ It is a place where prodigals come home . . .
✓ Where chains fall off . . .
✓ Where what is wrong is made right . . .
✓ Where the crooked is made straight . . .
✓ Where the rough edges are made smooth . . .
✓ Where desert desolations are turned to oases . . .
✓ Where ancient ruins are repaired and restored . . .
✓ Where the power of sin is broken, even generationally . . .
✓ Where Jesus is magnified and lifted up . . .
✓ Where the Holy Spirit abides in power and authority . . .
✓ Where the saints realize who they are and what they have been equipped with . . .
✓ Where Satan and his minions can't stay!

This is the place called Dwell. It is the place where I want to perpetually live.

What about you?

Twenty-three. What powerful words!

Let us thank God for these priceless and powerful promises.

Let us further walk in these invaluable promises for our lives.

They are as sure as the very God who knows your name.

Notes

www.ingramcontent.com/pod-product-compliance
Lightning Source LLC
Chambersburg PA
CBHW071104090426
42737CB00013B/2480

* 9 7 8 1 6 8 4 8 8 0 6 4 5 *